Countries Around the World

Cuba

Frank Collins

Heinemann
LIBRARY

Chicago, Illinois

www.heinemannraintree.com

Visit our website to find out more information about Heinemann-Raintree books.

To order:

☎ Phone 888-454-2279

▣ Visit www.heinemannraintree.com to browse our catalog and order online.

Edited by Louise Galpine and Megan Cotugno
Designed by Ryan Frieson
Original illustrations © Capstone Global Library, Ltd., 2012
Illustrated by Oxford Designers & Illustrators
Picture research by Tracy Cummins
Originated by Capstone Global Library, Ltd.
Printed in China by China Translation and Printing Services

15 14 13 12
10 9 8 7 6 5 4 3 2

Library of Congress Cataloging-in-Publication Data
Collins, Frank.
 Cuba / Frank Collins.
   p. cm.—(Countries around the world)
 Includes bibliographical references and index.
 ISBN 978-1-4329-5199-3 (hc)—ISBN 978-1-4329-5224-2 (pb)
 1. Cuba—Juvenile literature. I. Title.
 F1758.5.C373 2012
 972.91—dc22   2010043179

Acknowledgments

The author and publishers are grateful to the following for permission to reproduce copyright material: © Alamy: pp. 19 (© Sami Sarkis), 20 (© Premaphotos); © AP Photo: p. 22 (© Jose Goitia/CANADIAN PRESS PHOTO); © Corbis: pp. 5 (© Patrick Escudero/Hemis), 31 (© STR/Reuters); © Getty Images: pp. 6 (Hulton Archive), 9 (Lee Lockwood//Time Life Pictures), 11, 24 (STR/AFP), 35 (STR/AFP); © istockphoto: pp. 23 (© PeterPhoto), 32 (© John Rodriguez); © Shutterstock: pp. 7 (© Zoran Karapancev), 13 (© robert paul van beets), 14 (© RoxyFer), 15 (© PHB.cz [Richard Semik]), 18 (© Johann Helgason), 21 (© donvictorio), 27 (© RoxyFer), 28 (© Hannamariah), 37 (© Kamira), 46 (© Fotogroove); ©SuperStock: p. 16 (© Prisma VWPics).

Cover photograph reproduced with permission of Getty Images (Angelo Cavalli).

We would like to thank Richard Abisla and Sarah Blue for their invaluable help in the preparation of this book.

Every effort has been made to contact copyright holders of any material reproduced in this book. Any omissions will be rectified in subsequent printings if notice is given to the publisher.

All the Internet addresses (URLs) given in this book were valid at the time of going to press. However, due to the dynamic nature of the Internet, some addresses may have changed, or sites may have changed or ceased to exist since publication. While the author and Publishers regret any inconvenience this may cause readers, no responsibility for any such changes can be accepted by either the author or the Publishers.

Contents

Some words in the book are in bold, **like this**. You can find out what they mean by looking in the glossary.

Introducing Cuba

What comes to mind when you think about Cuba? Is it Fidel Castro, cigars, and classic cars? Or is it beaches and rhythmic music? The island nation of Cuba is all of these things, but also much more.

Cuba's official name is the Republic of Cuba, or *República de Cuba*, in Spanish, the official language. It is about the size of Kentucky and includes one large island and hundreds of small islands. These islands form part of a larger chain called the Antilles, or **West Indies**.

Cuba is the largest island nation in the Caribbean. It is long and narrow, running northwest to southeast. It is located just south of the **Tropic of Cancer** and has a warm, **tropical climate**. About one-fourth of Cuba is covered in mountains and hills, and the lowlands are good for farming. Cuba sits where three major bodies of water meet: the Atlantic Ocean, Caribbean Sea, and Gulf of Mexico. Cuba's nearest neighbors are Haiti, Jamaica, the Bahamas, and the United States. All of these countries are within 150 kilometers (90 miles) of Cuba.

Cuba is known for its unique culture—including its music, dance, and food—and its commitment to education and health care. Despite many difficult times, the culture and spirit of the Cuban people remains firm.

How to say...

Bienvenidos a Cuba is Spanish and means "Welcome to Cuba."

Cuba is known for its many beaches and colorful, classic automobiles.

History: Colonial Rule and Revolution

Around 4000 BCE, the Guanahatabey and Ciboney peoples, who probably came from South America, lived in Cuba. The Guanahatabey were the first tobacco farmers in Cuba. The Taíno people arrived around 500 CE, also from South America. The Taíno were farmers, but also fished and hunted. About 90 percent of Cubans were Taíno when European explorer Christopher Columbus arrived in 1492. Columbus had set sail for India, but landed in Central America instead.

Spanish conquest

Columbus landed in Cuba on his first voyage and claimed it for Spain. Spanish **conquistadors** came in the early 1500s, bringing African slaves with them. The Spanish used force to control the native peoples of Cuba, and were often cruel. By 1550 many of the native peoples had died because they had no **immunity** to European diseases.

The harbor at Havana in Cuba became an important stopping point between Spain and its American **colonies**. Sugar was grown on **plantations** using slaves. As the sugar industry grew, so did the population. By 1860 Cuba had more than 1.3 million people, and almost half were slaves.

Struggle for independence

Many Cubans wanted independence and began a war against Spain. At the end of the **Ten Years' War** (1868–1878), Spain promised to make changes in Cuba. Slavery was ended in 1886, but other promises were broken. Fighting started again in 1895.

When he arrived, Columbus thought Cuba was part of the Asian continent.

JOSÉ MARTÍ

(1853–1895)

José Martí was banished to Spain in 1871 for opposing its rule in Cuba. He fled his exile and went to New York City. Martí planned the next war and led the fighting. He was killed and became the symbol of Cuba's struggle for independence.

United States occupation

Spain was brutal in its fight against the **rebels**. Tens of thousands died of starvation and disease in prison camps. Both sides killed civilians and destroyed property. **Yellow journalism** in United States newspapers created anti-Spanish feelings.

In February 1898, the ship *USS Maine* sank in Havana's harbor after an unexplained explosion. The United States quickly decided to help the Cubans fight the Spanish and soon won. But instead of giving Cuba its independence, the United States took control of Cuba for four years.

Republic of Cuba

The independent Republic of Cuba formed in 1902. The United States only handed over power to the new Cuban government after it agreed to give the Americans the right to build a naval base at Guantánamo Bay. Cuba prospered from sugar and American tourism in the early 1900s. However, Cuban leaders became **corrupt**.

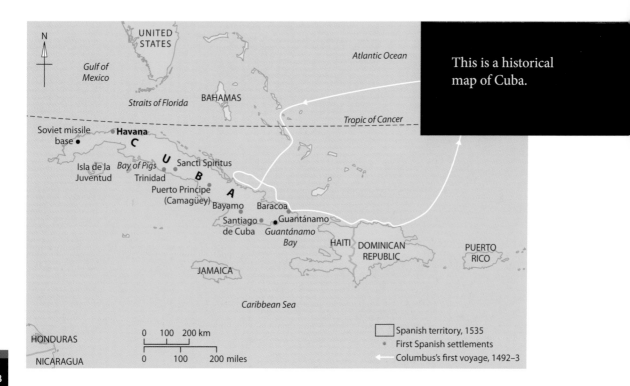

This is a historical map of Cuba.

Cuban president Fulgencio Batista (1901–1973) became a brutal **dictator** in the 1950s. Forces led by Fidel Castro invaded Cuba from Mexico in 1956 to fight Batista. The invasion failed, but Fidel Castro, his brother Raúl, and Che Guevara escaped and hid in the mountains. They organized sneak attacks against Batista's forces. When Batista fled in 1959, Fidel Castro took over.

DR. ERNESTO "CHE" GUEVARA
(1928–1967)

Che Guevara was from Argentina. He joined Fidel and Raúl Castro in Mexico and helped them overthrow Batista. Guevara was killed in South America fighting in another war for independence. Guevara's image became a symbol for **revolutionaries** worldwide.

Che Guevara (right) was photographed here with Raúl Castro (left) in 1964 while celebrating the revolution.

Fidel Castro's government

At this time, the United States was involved in the **Cold War** against the Soviet Union. The new Cuban government was modeled on the **communist** Soviet Union and became its partner. The United States found this threatening and declared a trade **embargo**. This stopped Americans from visiting or trading with Cuba and banned Cuban goods from being sold in the United States.

From 1959 to 1962, Castro had thousands of opponents imprisoned or killed. Hundreds of thousands of Cubans fled to the United States. In 1961 some anti-Castro Cuban **refugees**, supported by the United States, led a failed invasion of Cuba at the Bay of Pigs. Then, in 1962, there was almost war when the United States discovered Soviet missiles on the way to Cuba. To end the Cuban Missile Crisis, the Soviet Union removed its missiles, and the United States promised not to invade Cuba.

The 1990s

Thousands of Cubans continued to flee to the United States each year. The collapse of the Soviet Union in 1991 created tough economic times in Cuba. The government had to make changes. It began to allow greater freedoms for its people.

Into the 21st century

In 2006, because of poor health, Fidel Castro handed over presidential power to his brother Raúl. He officially resigned in 2008, and Raúl Castro was elected as Cuba's new president. The government lifted its ban on the ownership of cell phones and computers. In 2009 U.S. President Barack Obama said he wanted a fresh start with Cuba.

A U.S. airplane flies on patrol over a Soviet freight ship in this 1962 photograph taken during the Cuban Missile Crisis.

Regions and Resources: An Island Nation

Cuba has more beaches than any country in the Caribbean, with twice as much coastline as California. There are caves in some shoreline cliffs that in the past served as hideouts for pirates, **rebels**, and escaped slaves. Cuba's coasts also have **coral reefs**.

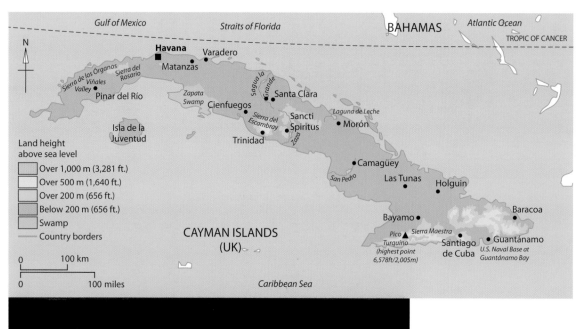

Cuba has a variety of landscapes, from beaches to mountains.

How to say...

Leche is Spanish for "milk." Cuba's largest lake, Laguna de la Leche ("Milky Lagoon") gets its name from its milky-white mineral waters. It is a small lake with a total surface area of 67.2 square kilometers (25.9 square miles).

The lay of the land

Cuba's other natural features include swamps, **lagoons**, rolling plains, forested hills, and even rugged mountains. The highest point is Pico Turquino at 2,005 meters (6,578 feet) in the Sierra Maestra mountains. Cuba's **tropical climate** gives it a rainy season from May to October. Hurricanes are a threat from August to November.

In the Viñales Valley, *mogotes* are rounded, rocky hills with thick vegetation. They remained after the softer **limestone** rock around them **eroded**. The hills in western Cuba are full of caves and underground rivers. The Santo Tomás cave system runs for 44 kilometers (25 miles). The Zapata Swamp is the largest wetland in the Caribbean, similar to the Everglades in Florida. It is home to the Cuban crocodile, which is rare and unique to Cuba.

Palm trees and rounded hills dot the landscape of Cuba's Viñales Valley.

The sea

As an island nation, the sea is one of Cuba's most important resources. Cuba's natural harbors and its location have made it an essential trade hub. Cuba's beaches and coral reefs draw tourists to the island who bring in a lot of money. Fishing is also an important industry. Cuba **exports** fish, shrimp, and lobsters.

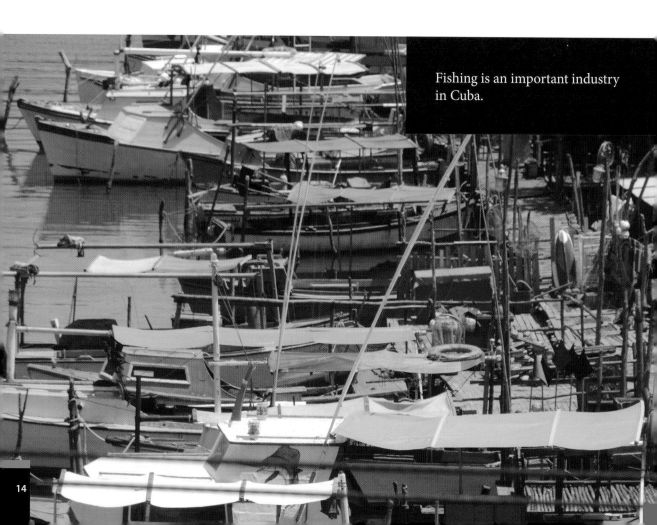

Fishing is an important industry in Cuba.

Cuba produces much of the world's sugar.

Farming

Cuba is no longer the world's greatest producer of sugar, but sugar is still an important export. Other crops include rice, potatoes, **plantains**, bananas, cassava, tomatoes, and corn. Tobacco is also grown. Some is used to make Cuba's famous hand-rolled cigars, which Cuba exports around the world. Cubans grow coffee, but most of it is consumed locally. Farmers grow fruits such as grapefruits, oranges, and pineapples for export.

Daily Life

Most farm work in Cuba is done by hand. Farmers in the hills hack down sugarcane using **machetes**. Tobacco farmers pick the leaves by hand, using knives. Instead of paying **income tax**, many Cubans from cities volunteer for agricultural work as their way of giving back to the government. Most Cuban teenagers are expected to work on a farm for several weeks each summer as their contribution.

Mining

Nickel, chromite, and copper is mined in Cuba. Cuba is a world leader in nickel production, which it exports after processing it in large plants. Nickel is often used in batteries. Cuba is also a leading producer of cobalt, a **byproduct** of nickel production. Cobalt is used to treat cancer, create blue paints, and create stronger alloys. Alloys are combinations of metals. Chromite is the source of chromium, which is used to make chrome hubcaps and bumpers. Copper is used to make wire. Cuba also **quarries** limestone, which is crushed and made into cement.

This Cuban mine produces nickel, which is an important export.

Tourism and services jobs

Over 60 percent of Cuban workers have jobs in the service industries. Service
jobs include government and tourism workers, teachers, bus drivers, and
doctors. Cuba relies a great deal on money from tourism. New hotels were
built in the 1990s to attract more tourists.

Many Cubans work in health care and education, which are available to all
people free of charge. Cuba also has free day care for children under seven.
With a free education, many of Cuba's best students train to become doctors.
Some of them now work in nearby countries where there is a shortage
of doctors.

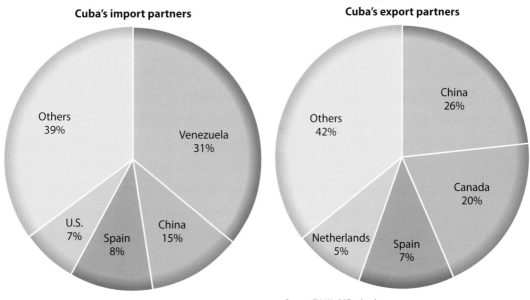

Cuba's import partners

Others 39%
Venezuela 31%
China 15%
Spain 8%
U.S. 7%

Source: U.S. Department of State Bureau of Western Hemisphere Affairs

Cuba's export partners

China 26%
Canada 20%
Others 42%
Spain 7%
Netherlands 5%

Source: CIA World Factbook

Wildlife: From Ceibas to Crocodiles

Cuba is a **tropical** island, with thousands of different plants and animals. The wild areas are very colorful, with many different flowering plants. Forests cover about one-fourth of Cuba. Many trees, plants, and animals are rare and found only in Cuba.

Habitats

Cuba has a large variety of **habitats**. There are jungles, grasslands, mountain forests, swamps, **coral reefs**, small islands, and patches of desert. The Zapata Swamp is in the western part of Cuba. This wetland is one of the world's most important **wildlife reserves**. Several kinds of plants and animals that live there are found only in the Zapata Swamp.

Cuban crocodiles are bred on this farm in order to better survive, and are then released into the Zapata Swamp.

The seeds of the ceiba tree are wrapped in a soft material which is harvested and used to stuff cushions.

Plant life

Cuba has a variety of trees, including palms, pines, and broad-leaved trees. The ceiba tree is one of Cuba's tallest trees, growing up to 60 meters (200 feet) high. Roots stick out of the trunk above the ground to support it as it grows. The ceiba tree is part of many Cuban legends.

The cork palms found in western Cuba are extremely rare. They are considered "living fossils," because they are a type of plant that has existed for more than 100 million years! Coastal mangrove forests make up one-third of Cuba's trees. The royal palm is Cuba's national tree. It is found all over the country and grows up to 23 meters (75 feet) tall.

Unique animals

Many animals exist only in Cuba. The solenodon is an almost-extinct mammal that looks like a rat. It has small eyes, a long tail, and a flexible snout that it uses to find insects to eat. The world's smallest frog was discovered in Cuba in 1993. Another rare animal is the tiny, painted snail.

The green-and-blue Cuban parrot was almost extinct, but is now protected and making a comeback. The red-white-and-blue tocororo, whose colors match the Cuban flag, is Cuba's national bird. The rare West Indian manatee swims in Cuba's shallow waters. Also called the sea cow, the typical manatee is about 3 meters (9.8 feet) long and weighs between 400 and 600 kilograms (900 to 1,300 pounds).

Cuba has unique snails, such as this painted tree snail.

How to say...

Cubans call the bee hummingbird *zunzuncito* (zoon-zoon-seetoh), meaning "little buzzer." It is the world's smallest bird, weighing less than a penny, and is found only in Cuba.

Environmental conservation

Cuba has tried hard to preserve its natural environment and resources. Since the 1990s, Cuba has practiced **sustainable** agriculture, growing **organic** fruits and vegetables. At the same time, Cuba established wildlife preserves, including Zapata Swamp. Cuba now has over 70 protected areas covering over 15 percent of the country.

YOUNG PEOPLE

UNESCO (United Nations Educational, Scientific and Cultural Organization) started the Sandwatch project in 1999. Groups of volunteer students and teachers in Cuba take part each year. They try to find solutions to pollution and other problems facing Cuba's beaches.

Cuba's coasts are an important habitat for flamingoes.

Infrastructure:
A Communist State

Cuba is a **communist** country. Communist states own all property and businesses and set all prices and pay. The Soviet Union was a powerful communist country and Cuba's main partner until it collapsed in 1991. Since then Cuba has faced tough times and has had to make some changes.

The government controls most parts of Cuban life. Since 1965, the Cuban Communist Party (the PCC) has been the only political party allowed. The Cuban president is the leader of the government and rules the country. Fidel Castro was president for 49 years. He resigned in 2008, and his brother, Raúl, became president.

The Castros have run Cuba for more than 50 years.

Cuba has two currencies, the national peso used by locals and the convertible peso used by visitors. The convertible peso is tied to the dollar.

Cuba's **legislature** is the National Assembly of the People's Power. Cuba is divided into 14 provinces and 170 municipalities. There are provincial and municipal assemblies with elected representatives. Any Cuban 16 years old or over can vote.

Transportation and technology

Because of prices and the United States trade **embargo**, it is difficult for Cubans to get new automobiles. Many Cubans have learned to repair classic 1950s cars. The oil that makes gasoline for the cars comes from Venezuela. Many Cubans use buses or bicycles.

Since 2008 the Cuban government has allowed people to buy computers, cell phones, and DVD players. However, most people can't afford their own computers, so they use them in schools and universities. The Cuban government limits access to the Internet.

Education

Education is free in Cuba at all levels, from preschool to college. The government also provides school supplies and meals. Cuba has a very high level of literacy (people who can read), and most Cubans are highly educated.

All Cuban children go to government public schools. There are no private schools. Cuban schoolchildren wear uniforms. There is a different color for each grade. Cuban children study typical school subjects, but also study their own country's history and English as a second language. Teenagers often study at **boarding schools** in the countryside for a time, where they help with farmwork.

These Cuban schoolchildren have red uniforms.

Daily Life

Cuban schoolchildren start the day standing and saluting the national flag while listening to the national anthem, *La Bayamesa*. It honors those who fought for Cuban independence and was first performed during the Battle of Bayamo in 1868. Some of the lyrics are: "Fear not a glorious death, because to die for the country is to live. To live in chains is to live in dishonor and shame."

Cuban children start elementary school at age 5 or 6, and finish at age 12. They then attend secondary school (high school) until age 16 or 17. Students who are not planning on going to college learn specific job skills at secondary school. After secondary school, many of the best students go to one of Cuba's universities.

Cuba's population by age (2010)

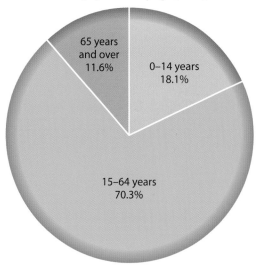

65 years and over 11.6%

0–14 years 18.1%

15–64 years 70.3%

Cuba's population by location (2008)

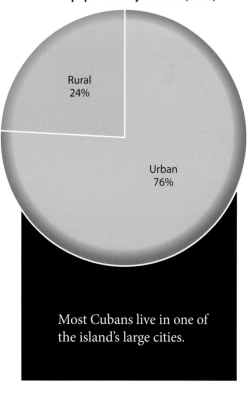

Rural 24%

Urban 76%

Source: CIA World Factbook

Most Cubans live in one of the island's large cities.

Health care

Cuba has about 59 doctors for every 10,000 people—far more than most countries. Doctors' services are free to all Cubans. They focus on preventing illnesses. Even though Cuba is known throughout the world for its excellent health care system, there is a shortage of some medical equipment and expensive medicines. International organizations and visiting tourists often donate medicines. Despite the shortages, many Cuban people are very healthy.

Daily Life

Cuba suffers from many shortages, including food. The government **rations** food. Through rationing, the government makes sure everyone gets a small amount and no one goes hungry. People then buy the rest of their food in the markets.

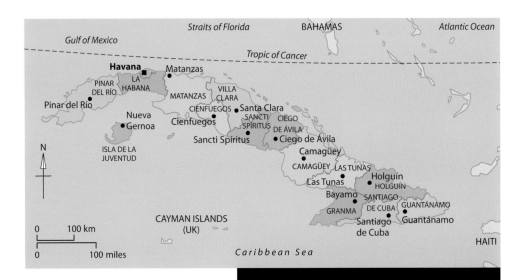

Cuba is divided into 14 provinces.

Recent changes

In 2009 Cuba celebrated the 50th anniversary of the Revolution of 1959. As it celebrated its past, Cubans enjoyed greater freedoms. More farmers now own some land and grow food to sell. Cubans also have greater access to technology, like computers and cell phones.

Housing

Cuban houses in small towns are usually made from concrete, brick, wood, and adobe (sun-dried mud bricks). Some old plantation mansions are split into several homes, but many are in bad condition. Some people in rural (country) areas live in *bohíos*. These small mud and clay houses are easy to build. Most city people live in plain concrete apartment buildings. The government built these to solve the housing shortage after the Revolution of 1959.

This is a view of historic Trinidad Street in Trinidad, Cuba.

Culture:
A Blend of Influences

Spanish, African, and native influences blend together in Cuba. The government supports Cuban culture through sports and the arts. Even small towns have cultural centers that display works from local artists and offer free music, art, drama, and dance instruction.

Music

Music is a huge part of Cuban culture. A type of music called *son* (sohn) was invented in Cuba over 200 years ago. Cuban music combines African drums and Spanish guitar. *Son* also features a Cuban guitar called a *tres* (trays) and the *claves* (klah-vays), which are wooden sticks hit together to beat out a rhythm.

Cuban bandleader Juan de Marcos González made *son* popular worldwide in 1997 through the album *Buena Vista Social Club*. Many popular styles of music and dance come from *son*, including rumba, mambo, and salsa.

These stilt walkers are celebrating **carnival** on Old Havana Street.

Religion

The Spanish brought **Catholicism** to Cuba. African slaves brought their own spiritual beliefs. Many Cubans practice *Santería*, which is a combination of the two. The **communist** government banned all religion. However, Christmas was made a holiday again in 2007 when the **pope** visited Cuba, and Cubans were granted more religious freedom.

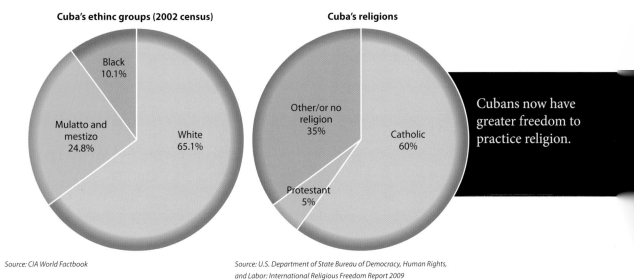

Cuba's ethinc groups (2002 census)

Black 10.1%

Mulatto and mestizo 24.8%

White 65.1%

Source: CIA World Factbook

Cuba's religions

Other/or no religion 35%

Catholic 60%

Protestant 5%

Source: U.S. Department of State Bureau of Democracy, Human Rights, and Labor: International Religious Freedom Report 2009

Cubans now have greater freedom to practice religion.

How to say...

A friendly Cuban greeting includes a light hug and kiss on the cheek. Cubans say "*buenos días!*" (bway-nohs dee-ahs), which means "hello" or "good day." Here are some other useful Spanish phrases:

good-bye	*adiós*	(ah-dee-ohs)
please	*por favor*	(pohr fah-vohr)
thank you	*gracias*	(grah-see-ahs)
it's nothing (you're welcome)	*de nada*	(day nah-dah)

Art and literature

Colorful Cuban art reflects the land and its people. Wilfredo Lam (1902–1982) was a famous Cuban painter whose work exhibited African influences. Cuba is also famous for its poster art, often of images from the 1959 revolution. Many Cubans love reading, and poetry is popular. Many Cubans also enjoy the poems of writer and national hero José Martí (see page 7).

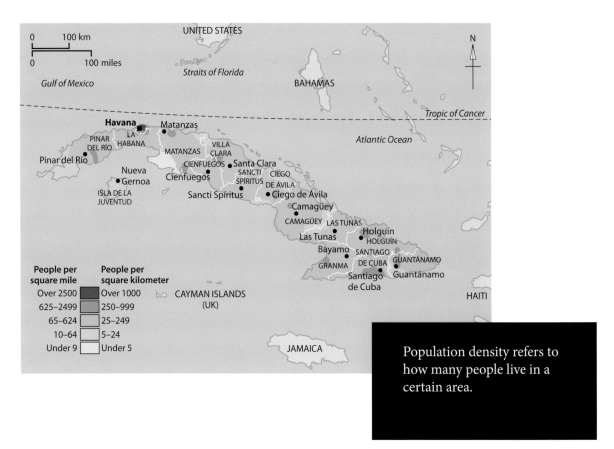

Population density refers to how many people live in a certain area.

Women in Cuba

Cuban women have equal legal rights. Most women work, and women make up almost half of Cuba's workforce. The government provides free day care to help families. Women also have equal opportunities in the military. A working woman's husband is required by law to do his share of housework and child care.

Young people dance as Cuba's salsa band Los Van Van performs during a concert in Havana in 2010.

Pop culture

Cuba's national television stations are controlled by the government. Sports broadcasts, especially baseball, are popular. Cubans also watch educational programs, *telenovelas*, movies, American TV shows, and news. *Telenovelas* are television dramas similar to American soap operas. *Telenovelas* from other countries in **Latin America** are also popular.

Many Cubans love going to the movies. There are favorite Cuban actors, such as Jorge Perugorra, also known as "Pichi." Perugorra became famous worldwide in *Fresa y Chocolate* ("Strawberry and Chocolate"). The film won first prize at the Havana Film Festival and was the first Cuban film nominated for an Academy Award.

YOUNG PEOPLE

At night, young people often gather at a *casa de la trova*, which is a mix between a dance and concert hall. Musicians often play there, and it is a popular hangout for teenagers on weekends.

Sports and recreation

Baseball is the most popular sport in Cuba. Before baseball was removed from the Olympics for 2012, the Cuban team won gold or silver in 1992, 1996, 2000, 2004, and 2008. Every Cuban school competes in a baseball league. Both young and old watch or play baseball on the weekends.

Boxing is popular, and more people are playing basketball. Cubans are much less interested in soccer than other countries in Latin America. Being an island nation, fishing is a favorite hobby among Cubans. Cubans of all ages love playing dominoes.

Food

Cuban food blends Spanish ideas with African and other influences. Pork, chicken, and seafood are also popular. Rice and beans are very common and popular. Other common foods are yuca (cassava), cucumbers, tomatoes, **plantains**, and cabbage. Yuca is a starchy root, like a potato. Cuban food is flavored using onions, garlic, tomatoes, limes, oregano, and cumin.

Plantains are available in some grocery stores. They look like large bananas. Fried plantains are pictured here.

A Cuban Recipe: Fried Plantains

Plantains are like bananas: they are green before they ripen, and turn black when really ripe. Fried green plantains, called *tostones* (tohs-tohn-ays), are eaten with meals. Black plantains are much sweeter when fried. Cubans sometimes eat them for dessert.

Ingredients:

- vegetable or corn oil for frying
- a plantain peeled and cut into about 1-inch (3-cm) slices
- salt or sugar

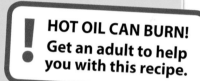

HOT OIL CAN BURN!
Get an adult to help you with this recipe.

Directions:

1. Fill a large skillet one-third full with oil and heat over medium-high heat

2. Once the oil is hot (about 300°F, or 167°C), fry the plantain slices for about 2–3 minutes on each side, until they are soft

3. Turn off the burner (but save the oil) and move the plantain slices onto paper towel

4. Wrap a brown paper bag around the bottom of a coffee cup and press/smash the plantains until they are about half their original thickness

5. Heat the oil again and fry the plantains until they are golden brown, turning them occasionally

7. Add salt or sugar. Serve and enjoy!

Cuba Today

President Raúl Castro began a program of government **reform** in 2008. After the election of President Barack Obama in 2008, the United States began to reconsider and loosen its trade **embargo**. Hurricanes in 2008 caused serious damage in Cuba. Facing tough times and the cost of repairing the damage, the Cuban government put further reforms on hold.

Cubans in Florida

Several hundred thousand Cuban refugees have settled in Florida since the revolution of 1959. Most settled in the city of Miami, where there is a district called Little Havana. Many Cuban-Americans have strong anti-Castro and anti-**communist** feelings. They want an end to communism in Cuba and want greater freedom for the island's people. But many Cubans in Florida hold on to their rich Cuban traditions and heritage.

Cuba after Castro

The Cuban people have kept their rich cultural traditions through many challenges and change. Who knows what will be in store for Cuba then? The certain thing is that Cuba and its people will remain unique in this amazing part of the world.

YOUNG PEOPLE

Young Cubans love getting a chance to hear musicians from outside the island. In 2009 the Cuban government allowed Colombian pop singer Juanes to organize a concert called "Peace Without Borders." Cuban musicians also took part. Over one million people attended the event in Havana's Plaza de la Revolución (Plaza of the Revolution).

Farmers sell food in open city markets, such as this one in Havana, to make money.

Fact File

Country Name: Republic of Cuba

Date of Independence: May 20, 1902 (not acknowledged by Cuban government)

Total Land Area: 109,820 square kilometers (42,400 square miles)

Climate: tropical

Average Temperature: 25°C (77°F)

Average High Temperature: 27.2°C (81°F)

Average Low Temperature: 21°C (70°F)

Average Yearly Rainfall: 1,320 millimeters (52 inches)

Highest Point: Pico Turquino—2,005 meters (6,578 feet)

Lowest Point: sea level—0 meters (0 feet)

Longest River: Cauto—370 kilometers (230 miles)

Largest Lake: Leche Lagoon—67 square kilometers (26 square miles)

Major Mountain Ranges: Sierra Maestra, Sierra del Escambray, Sierra de los Órganos, Sierra del Rosario

Major Rivers: Cauto, Sagua la Grande, Zaza

Population: 11,451,652 (2010 est.)

Language: Spanish

Literacy Rate: 99.8%

El Morro castle in Havana's harbor was built in the 1590s to protect against pirates.

Life Expectancy: 77.45 years

Government: communist (socialist republic)

Capital: Havana

Gross Domestic Product: $110.9 billion (2009 est.)

Currency: peso (100 centavos = 1 peso)

Resources: nickel, cobalt, chromium, copper

Industries: tourism, sugar, tobacco, nickel, fish

Trade Partners: China, Canada, Spain, and the Netherlands

Unemployment Rate: 1.7% (2009 est.)

Main Exports: sugar, nickel, tobacco, fish, citrus fruit

Main Imports: petroleum, food, machinery, chemicals

National Symbols:	bird	tocororo
	tree	royal palm
	flower	butterfly jasmine, white mariposa

National Holidays:

January 1	Liberation Day (celebrating Revolution of 1959)
May 1	International Workers' Day
July 25–27	National Rebellion Day (remembers Castro's attack in 1953 that began the revolution); also Carnival since 1998
October 10	Anniversary of start of First War of Independence in 1868
December 25	Christmas Day (restored as a public holiday in 1997)

Famous Cubans:

Orlando "El Duque" Hernández (b. 1965), baseball player
Alicia Alonso (b. 1920), ballet dancer
Raúl Martínez (1927–1995), artist
Alejo Carpentier (1904–1980), writer
José Lezama Lima (1910–1976), poet
Nicolás Guillén (1902–1989), poet
Compay Segundo (1907–2003), musician
Fulgencio Batista, (1901–1973), dictator
Fidel Castro (b. 1926), president
Celia Cruz (1924–2003), singer
Wilfredo Lam (1902–1982), artist
José Martí (1853–1895), revolutionary and writer
Carlos Manuel de Céspedes (1819–1874), revolutionary
Antonio Maceo (1845–1896), revolutionary
Jorge Perugorria (b. 1965), actor
Silvio Rodriguez (b. 1946), singer
Javier Sotomayor (b. 1967), olympic athlete

National Parks: Ciénaga de Zapata National Park (Zapata Swamp)
Viñales National Park
Desembarco del Granma National Park
Turquino National Park
Pico Cristal National Park
Alejandro de Humboldt National Park

Cuban National Anthem: "La Bayamesa"
Hasten to battle, men of Bayamo,
For the homeland looks proudly to you.
Fear not a glorious death,
Because to die for the country is to live.

To live in chains
Is to live in dishonor and shame.
Hear the clarion call,
Hasten, brave ones, to battle!

Timeline

BCE means "before the common era." When this appears after a date, it refers to the number of years before the Christian religion began. BCE dates are always counted backward.

CE means "common era." When this appears after a date, it refers to the time after the Christian religion began.

BCE

c. 4000	Ciboney and Guanahatabey people settle in Cuba

CE

c. 500	Taíno people arrive in Cuba and slowly push out most of the Ciboney and Guanahatabey
1492	Christopher Columbus arrives in Cuba and claims it for Spain
1511	Spanish conquistador Diego Velásquez de Cuéllar begins settlement of Cuba with 300 Spaniards and their African slaves
1791	Black slaves in Haiti rebel; some Haitian planters escape to Cuba, where the sugar trade continues to grow
1868–1878	**Ten Years' War,** in which Cuban revolutionaries fight Spanish rule
1886	Slavery is abolished in Cuba
1895	Poet José Martí helps lead a revolt against Spanish rule and is killed while fighting
1898	Spanish-American War, in which the United States supports Cuban revolutionaries and easily defeats Spain
1899–1902	The United States rules Cuba
1902	The Republic of Cuba is founded
1903	The United States establishes a military base at Guantánamo in Cuba

1952	Fulgencio Batista takes control of the Cuban government
1956	Fidel Castro and his forces begin a revolution against the Cuban government
1959	Batista flees the country and Fidel Castro takes control of the Cuban government, which is made similar to the communist Soviet Union
1959–1963	Major migration of Cuban refugees to the United States
1960	The United States places an economic embargo on Cuba
1961	Cubans trained by the United States invade Cuba at the Bay of Pigs and are quickly defeated by the Cuban military forces
1962	The United States forces the Soviet Union to remove its nuclear missiles from Cuba after what is known as the Cuban Missile Crisis
1976	A new constitution establishes the Communist Party as the only political party in Cuba
1991	Cuba's closest trading partner, the Soviet Union, collapses, and Cuba's economy begins to suffer
1993	The communist Cuban government allows some Cubans to start privately owned businesses
1994	Cuban refugees try to migrate to the United States in Balsero Crisis
1998	Pope John Paul II visits Cuba; Cubans are given more religious freedom
2006	While recovering from surgery, Fidel Castro hands over power to his brother, Raúl
2008	Fidel Castro officially resigns, and Raúl Castro becomes the new president of Cuba; government lifts ban on ownership of cell phones and computers; in September Hurricanes Gustav and Ike cause the worst storm damage in Cuba's history
2009	United States President Barack Obama says he wants a new beginning with Cuba

Glossary

boarding school school where students live and study

byproduct something additional that is produced during a process

carnival public event at which people play music, wear special clothes, and dance in the streets

Catholicism religion of the Roman Catholic Church

climate usual weather conditions of a particular area

Cold War unfriendly relationship between the United States and Soviet Union between the end of World War II (1945) and the collapse of the Soviet Union in 1991

colony country or area under the control of a more powerful country, which is usually far away

communist relating to communism, a political system where the government owns and controls the property and businesses

conquistador 1500s Spanish soldier

coral reef often colorful line of hard rocks formed by coral, found in the sea

corrupt using power in a dishonest way in order to benefit yourself

dictator ruler who has complete power over a country and keeps it by force, or the threat of force

embargo official order to stop trade with a country

eroded when a surface is gradually worn away by the weather

export something sold to or sent to another country, or the act of doing so

habitat natural home of a plant or animal

immunity state of being protected from a particular disease

income tax tax paid to the government on money you earn

lagoon small lake of sea water that is partly separated from the sea

Latin America countries of the Americas and Caribbean where Spanish and Portuguese are spoken

legislature lawmaking body of government

limestone rock that contains the mineral calcium

machete large knife with a wide, heavy blade

organic relating to methods of growing food without using artificial chemicals

plantain large kind of banana that is cooked before eaten

plantation large farm where crops such as sugar, tobacco, or cotton are grown, often using slaves as workers

pope head of the Catholic Church

quarry dig stone or sand from a place; also the place people dig stone or sand from

ration control the supply of something because there is not enough

rebel someone who fights against people in authority

reform improve something by making changes; also the change itself that is meant to improve things

refugee someone who has been forced to leave their country

revolutionary someone who supports a revolution

sustainable able to continue for a long time without causing damage to the environment

Ten Years' War war in which Cuba fought for independence from Spain

Tropic of Cancer line of latitude 23°27′ north

tropical from or existing in the warmest parts of the world

West Indies islands of the Caribbean Sea, including The Bahamas, Cuba, Jamaica, Puerto Rico, Barbados, and Dominica

wildlife reserve area of land set aside for the protection of animals, plants, and habitats

yellow journalism journalism that exaggerates or even lies in the news it reports in order to create excitement and attract readers

Find Out More

Books

Cavallo, Anna. *Cuba (Country Explorers)*. Minneapolis: Lerner Publications, 2011.

Doak, Robin S. *Cuba (First Reports)*. Minneapolis: Compass Point, 2004.

Donovan, Sandy. *Teens in Cuba (Global Connections)*. Minneapolis: Compass Point, 2009.

Green, Jen. *Cuba (Countries of the World)*. Washington, D.C.: National Geographic, 2007.

Sheen, Barbara. *Foods of Cuba (A Taste of Culture)*. Detroit: Kidhaven Press, 2010.

Tracy, Kathleen. *We Visit Cuba (Your Land and My Land)*. Hockessin, Del.: Mitchell Lane Publishers, 2010.

Websites

www.moma.org/collection/object.php?object_id=34666
You can see and read about Cuban artist Wilfredo Lam's famous painting called The Jungle on this website.

www.cia.gov/library/publications/the-world-factbook/geos/cu.html
The World Factbook is a publication of the Central Intelligence Agency (CIA) of the United States. It provides information on Cuba and over 250 other nations.

http://portal.unesco.org/science/en/ev.php-URL_ID=5741&URL_DO=DO_TOPIC&URL_SECTION=201.html
Learn about Cuba's involvement with the United Nations Educational, Scientific and Cultural Organization (UNESCO) in maintaining coastal regions.

www.who.int/countries/cub/en/
The World Health Organization (WHO) provides health information concerning Cuba.

www.prb.org/Datafinder/Geography/Summary.aspx?region=87&region_type=2
The Population Reference Bureau website provides a lot of data on Cuba's population and other features.

http://unstats.un.org/unsd/default.htm
This United Nations site offers links to a range of statistics on Cuba and other countries.

Places to visit

Havana
This is the historic capital of Cuba.

Valle de Viñales
These are limestone cliffs and caves in western Cuba.

Ciénaga de Zapata
This is Cuba's largest wilderness area and includes the Zapata Swamp, which has rare types of plants and animals.

Trinidad
This historic city was declared a World Heritage site in 1988.

Santiago de Cuba
Cuba's second-largest city, located in eastern Cuba, has a thriving culture. It is the area where son music got its start.

Topic Tools

You can use these topic tools for your school projects. Trace the flag and map on to a sheet of paper, using the thick black outlines to guide you, then color in your pictures. Make sure you use the right colors for the flag!

The Cuban flag was first flown in 1850 by Cubans opposed to Spanish rule. Blue stripes represent the ocean surrounding Cuba and the three areas of Cuba in 1850. The white stripes stand for purity and independence. The red triangle represents the blood shed by revolutionaries and the white star represents liberty.

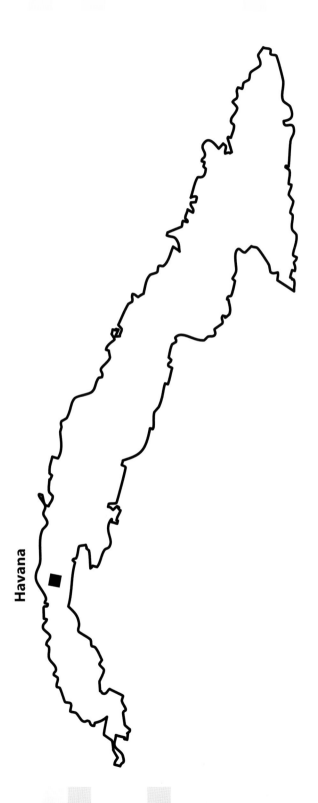

Havana

Index

Titles in the series